Stuff It!
Leave Boxed Stuffing Behind Forever

Gina Lynn

Synchron8 Publishing
www.synchron8publishing.com

ISBN Number: 978-1-942535-02-7 (eBook)
ISBN Number: 978-1-942535-03-4 (Paperback)

Disclaimer and Terms of Use: Effort has been made to ensure that the information in this book is accurate and complete; however, the author and the publisher do not warrant the accuracy of the information, text and graphics contained within the book due to the differences in cooking conditions. The Author and the publisher do not hold any responsibility for errors, omissions or contrary interpretation of the subject   matter   herein.

Thank You!

While I love all types of foods, drinks and cooking experiences, my mission is to provide readers with creative and satisfying recipes in a way that is valuable to them. My motto is "Quick, Handy, and Helpful" when it comes to my books. I recognize that there are a variety of options for finding dinner and other meal ideas, and I appreciate the fact that you have decided to purchase this book. As an added thank you, I am offering a free gift to you, my readers. With this book, you can receive a free bonus material not included here. The options in the bonus are just as tasty as the ones featured in this book (though some may argue the extras are even better). It is simply a way of saying thank you for your support.

To get the free, bonus collection of stuffing material, visit:

www.synchron8publishing.com/GLStuffIt

I hope you enjoy the yummy goodness ahead. When you are done, don't forget to leave a review for others who might benefit from the book. It doesn't take much, even if it's just a note on which recipe is your new favorite. It is much appreciated, and once again, thank you!

Table of Contents

Introduction

While holiday meals often highlight family favorites, sometimes the occasion calls for something new. Regardless of which holiday meal that you are preparing *Stuff It! Leave Boxed Stuffing Behind Forever* will give you 30 ideas for freshening up any holiday feast.

When we say any holiday meal, we do mean ANY holiday. Unlike other holiday recipe cooks, this book is designed to be useful year-around. It doesn't matter if you are preparing a Thanksgiving feast with turkey, a Christmas meal with beef roast, an Easter ham, or any gathering. We have targeted all types of holiday meals. Several of the recipes are vegetarian or vegan fare for those in your party who choose to skip the meat.

Many recipes will mention which main dishes work best with the given recipe, but there is nothing stopping you from mixing and matching as you see fit. So, if there is a recipe that notes that the stuffing works especially well with turkey, don't be afraid to try it with ham or other main courses if it sounds interesting to you. After all, it's your party, right?

My motto in creating these books is to be quick, handy, and helpful. While the vast majority of recipes adhere to this motto, a handful of them are a little more time intensive. When that is the case, the recipe description will note a longer prep and/or cooking time.

The goal for this book is to provide a resource that can be useful throughout the year. Even when you aren't preparing a holiday meal, the recipes can be used to pep up a weekly gathering or even a mid-week meal.

I hope you find it a useful tool for all of your holiday meal magic, and please feel free to drop me a note about your favorites on Twitter @GinaLynnYummies. I love to hear from my readers and fellow cooks! Happy eating!

Stuffing vs. Dressing

It is an ongoing and common debate...what constitutes a stuffing? What constitutes a dressing? I'm not sure if there's ever going to be a definitive answer to those questions.

For some, the difference is the result of how the dish is cooked. In this case, a stuffing is cooked within the cavity of a turkey, chicken or other meat. Conversely, a dressing is cooked separately and served as a side dish. Personally, I've never been a fan of actually cooking stuffing inside of a turkey (though I have done stuffed pork chops and salmon) simply because you need to be extra careful and vigilant about cooking temperatures in order to avoid nasty surprises after the meal is consumed. With that said, I personally still call the made-outside-the-meat dish, 'stuffing' anyway.

Another method for determining whether your dish is a stuffing or a dressing hinges on geography. It's the old North versus South situation. In the North and most of the West, 'stuffing' is the generally used and accepted term for the dish, regardless of how it is cooked. For those most typically in the South, the reverse is true and all dishes are referred to as dressings.

For our sake, we aren't going to fuel an old Civil War rivalry or debate the merits of how to cook a stuffing or dressing. In this book, the distinction is tied to the main ingredients. If the dish is bread-based, it will be categorized as a stuffing. For dishes that highlight rice, pasta or other grains, they are featured in the dressings version of this book: *Holiday Dressings: Leave the Bread Behind.*

For Vegetarians & Vegans

I have prepared and served countless holiday meals over the years, and that includes meals for those who don't eat meat. While it can seem to be a challenge to fix a meatless meal for holiday feasts where meat viewed as an eatable centerpiece, it really doesn't have to be that difficult. Again, I'm all about being handy and helpful, so there's no need to add more stress to your holiday preparations.

There are a variety of recipes featured in this book that are vegetarian and vegan oriented. The recipe descriptions include a note as to which recipes are vegan as opposed to vegetarian. The dishes can be served either as sides or in many cases an entree for those who prefer to skip the meat and/or other dairy products.

Bread Preparation

Before we launch into your options for creating delectable stuffing dishes, we must first address the notion of preparing your bread to be used in a stuffing recipe. If you use fresh bread in your stuffing recipe, the dish will be mush by the time it is ready to be served. To keep the consistency pleasant, you must first prepare your bread for use. There are three ways in which you can do this. The first two options are the most favorable, but the third option can work for those in a real pinch concerning cooking time.

Natural Air-Dried Bread Cubes

This is the most classic and traditional option for drying out your cubes of bread. While it is by far the easiest, it does require some planning to allow for time to take its course. Realistically, this process can take 24-72 hours, depending on how humid your environment is at the time. More humidity means that the drying out process will take longer. However, regardless of the moisture in the air you can speed up the time necessary if you begin with bread that is already going stale. (Plus, this practice saves on food waste, which was one of the reasons stuffing was created in the first place.)

The process is simple. For approximately 4 cups of dried bread cubes, use 4-5 slices of bread. (Many of the stuffing recipes call for 16 cups of bread cubes which equals 16-20 slices of bread cut into cubes) Adjust the amount of bread accordingly to the size of your planned stuffing dish. Cut the bread into cubes of the desired size (crust or no crust is a personal preference). Ideally, you should spread the bread cubes across a cookie sheet to maximize the contact with air to dry them all. A large bowl will work as well, but you will need to stir it regularly (every few hours) to be sure that the cubes dry out more evenly. It is best to leave the bread uncovered to speed up the drying.

You will know when your bread is ready to use when the outside has a texture that is similar to a crouton and there is minimal sponginess when you squeeze a bread cube.

Oven-Dried Bread Cubes

Basically, you are creating plain croutons when you oven-dry bread cubes. The process is similar for preparing the bread for the oven, and the actual drying process is shortened to 10-15 minutes. The tradeoff is the use of your oven.

Begin by pre-heating your oven to 300 degrees. Cut the desired amount of bread into cubes and spread across a cookie sheet or a large baking dish as a single layer. Bake for 10-15 minutes, stirring the cubes twice while baking. Allow cubes to cool. As they cool, they will continue to dry. As many recipes call for 16 cups of bread cubes, you may need to use more than one dish or cookie sheet to maintain a single layer of cubes while baking.

Store-Bought Dried Bread Cubes

If you want to skip the whole bread cube drying process, dried bread cubes are available in most grocery stores. The location of bread cubes in the store may vary, but it is mostly commonly found in the baking aisles.

For the Gluten-Sensitive

For those with gluten sensitivities, the most favorable options may be the dressings in the subsequent title rather than the stuffings in this book. While the stuffing recipes in this book are bread-based, those who have sensitivity to gluten can modify the recipes to enjoy the favorite holiday dish. Gluten-free breads are becoming increasingly common in grocery stores. They are typically found in the frozen foods/breads section because they use little or none of the preservatives found in breads on the shelf.

Due to the differences in gluten-free bread storage and the lack of preservatives, preparing bread cubes for stuffing is best done with the oven method. It is important to bring the bread to room temperature first, and baking times may be lengthened due to the bread's density.

Stuffings

This book features 30 stuffing recipes from classic and basic stuffing recipes, to richer and heartier options for stuffing that can suit the full range of holiday meal options. Once again, for our purposes here, a stuffing is defined within this book as a dish that features a bread component. Some stuffings can be created using any type of bread, while others use a specific kind of bread for a desired flavor profile. For those that do not specify a type of bread, you can use any white or wheat bread. To add to the eye appeal of your stuffing, you can also use a combination of both white and darker breads. For the best results a firmer style of bread is preferred to a softer one.

The first subsection of stuffing recipes include options that are vegetarian-friendly and do not contain meat. Two other subsections of recipes are dedicated to stuffings that include meat products. The first set of meat stuffing recipes includes sausage in the traditional sense. The second section of meaty stuffing recipes uses meat products other than the traditional   sausage.

Meat-Less Stuffing Recipes

This selection of stuffing recipes begins with the two basic stuffing recipes that comprise the base for the majority of recipes in this book. The classic recipe is targeted for use with white and darker wheat bread cubes. The second recipe is for a sweeter, cornbread stuffing base.

These recipes do include dairy and egg products, so vegans will need to follow the final recipe as a base. It is designed specifically for vegans, and the vegetarian recipes can then incorporate other vegetable options. The meatless stuffings can then be modified to vegan-fare. (Note: When doing modifications, butter will be substituted with vegetable or olive oil in any additional cooking steps beyond the vegan classic stuffing.)

Classic Stuffing

Forget the boxed stuff forever! This is a simple, traditional, and universal version of stuffing which serves as a base for the majority of the stuffing recipes in this book. This recipe results in approximately 8 servings.

Note: When using sourdough bread cubes, you may want to add rosemary with the other spices to enhance the flavor. Use rosemary sparingly as it is a pungent herb. I recommend chopping the rosemary for a finer consistency and using no more than 2 teaspoons.

You will need:

1 large skillet
1 large mixing bowl
1 large baking dish

Ingredients

1 Stick unsalted butter (plus butter to coat baking dish and dot the top with)
2 cups onions, diced
2 cups celery, diced
1 tablespoon sage, minced (or 2 teaspoons of dried sage)

1 tablespoon thyme, minced (or 2 teaspoons of dried thyme)
Salt and pepper to taste
3 cups broth (chicken, turkey, vegetable as preferred)
2 eggs
1/4 cup parsley, chopped
16 cups of dried bread cubes

Directions

Preheat oven to 375 degrees.

Melt 1 stick of butter in a large skillet over medium heat.
Add onions, celery, sage and thyme plus salt and pepper.
Cook 5 minutes on medium/low heat.
Add your choice of broth and bring to a simmer.

In a large bowl, beat 2 eggs and mix in parsley.
Add bread cubes. Pour in the vegetable mixture from the skillet and toss.
Transfer to a buttered baking dish and dot the top with butter.
Cover with foil and bake 30 minutes.
Uncover and continue baking until golden (approximately an additional 30 minutes).

Note: If you want to finish cooking the stuffing inside of a turkey or other meat, do so after the first 30 minutes of covered baking.

Classic Cornbread Stuffing

This classic cornbread stuffing actually uses a combination of cornbread cubes and white bread cubes in order to maintain a firmer consistency after baking. The added sweetness of cornbread is a pleasant taste to balance savory dishes and provides an approachable contrast to saltier and spicier additions in later recipes. This recipe results in approximately 8 servings.

You will need:

1 large skillet
1 large mixing bowl
1 large baking dish

Ingredients

1 stick of unsalted butter (plus butter to coat baking dish and dot the top with)
2 cups onions, diced
2 cups celery, diced
1 tablespoon sage, minced (or 2 teaspoons of dried sage)
1 tablespoon thyme (or 2 teaspoons of dried thyme)
Salt and pepper to taste
3 cups broth (chicken, turkey, vegetable as preferred)

2 eggs
1/4 cup parsley, chopped
6 cups of cornbread cubes, dried
8 cups of white bread cubes, dried

Directions

Preheat oven to 375 degrees.

Melt stick of butter in a large skillet over
  medium heat.
Add onions, celery, sage and thyme plus
  salt and pepper.
Cook 5 minutes on medium/low heat.
Add your choice of broth and bring to a
  simmer.

In a large bowl, beat 2 eggs and mix in
  parsley.
Add all bread cubes.
Pour in the vegetable mixture from the
  skillet and toss.
Transfer to a buttered baking dish and
  dot the top with butter.
Cover with foil and bake 30 minutes.
Uncover and continue baking until
  golden (approximately an additional
  30 minutes).

Apple-licious Classic Stuffing

Bring some of the flavor of fall harvest into your stuffing. This is stuffing works especially well with holiday ham, but it is a solid compliment to turkey as well. The recipe uses the classic stuffing recipe as a base and adds apple to the mix. Personally, I prefer to use Gala or Golden Delicious apples, but the choice is yours. If you want additional sweetness, you can also add a 1/2 cup of raisons in the final mixing step.

You will need:

1 large skillet
1 large mixing bowl
1 large baking dish

Ingredients

1 Stick unsalted butter (plus butter to coat baking dish and dot the top with)
2 cups onions, diced
2 cups celery, diced
2 medium to large apples, diced (approximately 2 cups)
1 tablespoon sage, minced (or 2 teaspoons of dried sage)
1 tablespoon thyme, minced (or 2 teaspoons of dried thyme)

Salt and pepper to taste

3 cups broth (chicken, turkey, vegetable as preferred)

2 eggs

1/4 cup parsley, chopped

16 cups of dried bread cubes

Directions

Preheat oven to 375 degrees.

Melt 1 stick of butter in a large skillet over medium heat.

Add onions, celery, apples, sage and thyme plus salt and pepper.

Cook 5 minutes on medium/low heat.

Add your choice of broth and bring to a simmer.

In a large bowl, beat 2 eggs and mix in parsley.

Add bread cubes. Pour in the vegetable mixture from the skillet and toss.

Transfer to a buttered baking dish and dot the top with butter.

Cover with foil and bake 30 minutes.

Uncover and continue baking until golden (approximately an additional 30 minutes).

Note: If you want to finish cooking the stuffing inside of a turkey or other meat, do so after the first 30 minutes of covered baking.

Cran-Apple Stuffing

While the Apple-licious Stuffing works best for ham dishes, this is the best apple flavored stuffing for turkey dishes, and combines the fall favorites for year-end holidays. For an additional flavor punch, add some freshly grated orange zest over the top when serving. This recipe uses the classic stuffing as a base and yields approximately 8 servings.

You will need:

1 large skillet
1 large mixing bowl
1 large baking dish

Ingredients

1 Stick unsalted butter (plus butter to coat baking dish and dot the top with)
2 cups onions, diced
2 cups celery, diced
2 medium to large apples diced (Gala or Golden Delicious)
1 cup dried cranberries
1 tablespoon sage, minced (or 2 teaspoons of dried sage)
1 tablespoon thyme, minced (or 2 teaspoons of dried thyme)

Salt and pepper to taste
3 cups broth (chicken, turkey, vegetable as preferred)
2 eggs
1/4 cup parsley, chopped
16 cups of dried bread cubes

Directions

Preheat oven to 375 degrees.

Melt 1 stick of butter in a large skillet over medium heat.
Add onions, celery, apples, cranberries, sage and thyme plus salt and pepper.
Cook 5 minutes on medium/low heat.
Add your choice of broth and bring to a simmer.

In a large bowl, beat 2 eggs and mix in parsley.
Add bread cubes. Pour in the vegetable mixture from the skillet and toss.
Transfer to a buttered baking dish and dot the top with butter.
Cover with foil and bake 30 minutes.
Uncover and continue baking until golden (approximately an additional 30 minutes).

Note: If you want to finish cooking the stuffing inside of a turkey or other meat, do so after the first 30 minutes of covered baking.

Apple Fennel Stuffing

Try this sophisticated version of cran-apple stuffing for meals with roasted beef and turkey. For more of an interesting flavor profile, try using potato bread for the cubes. Instead of using onion, this recipe features fennel for a hint of Italian influence in your holiday meal. This recipe results in approximately 8 servings.

You will need:

1 large skillet
1 large mixing bowl
1 large baking dish

Ingredients

1 Stick unsalted butter (plus butter to coat baking dish and dot the top with)
2 cups onions, diced
1 bulb fennel, diced (approximately 2 cups)
1 medium apple, diced
1 cup dried cranberries
1 tablespoon sage, minced (or 2 teaspoons of dried sage)
1 tablespoon thyme, minced (or 2 teaspoons of dried thyme)
Salt and pepper to taste

3 cups broth (chicken, turkey, vegetable
as preferred)
2 eggs
1/4 cup parsley, chopped
16 cups of dried bread cubes

Directions

Preheat oven to 375 degrees.

Melt 1 stick of butter in a large skillet
over medium heat.
Add onions, fennel, apples, cranberries,
sage and thyme plus salt and pepper.
Cook 5 minutes on medium/low heat.
Add your choice of broth and bring to a
simmer.

In a large bowl, beat 2 eggs and mix in
parsley.
Add bread cubes. Pour in the vegetable
mixture from the skillet and toss.
Transfer to a buttered baking dish and
dot the top with butter.
Cover with foil and bake 30 minutes.
Uncover and continue baking until
golden (approximately an additional
30 minutes).

Note: If you want to finish cooking the stuffing inside of a turkey or other meat, do so after the first 30 minutes of covered baking.

Nutty-Apricot Stuffing

This nutty and fruity stuffing is great with a full range of entrees. A mix of toasted nuts can make the stuffing uniquely your own with the use of hazelnuts, walnuts, almonds or pecans. The classic stuffing foundation results in approximately 8 servings.

You will need:

1 large skillet
1 large mixing bowl
1 large baking dish

Ingredients

1 Stick unsalted butter (plus butter to coat baking dish and dot the top with)
2 cups leeks, diced
2 cups celery, diced
1 tablespoon sage, minced (or 2 teaspoons of dried sage)
1 tablespoon thyme, minced (or 2 teaspoons of dried thyme)
Salt and pepper to taste
3 cups broth (chicken, turkey, vegetable as preferred)
2 eggs
1/4 cup parsley, chopped
16 cups of dried bread cubes

1 cup toasted nuts (personal preference)
1 1/2 cups dried apricots, diced

Directions

Preheat oven to 375 degrees.

Melt 1 stick of butter in a large skillet
over medium heat.
Add leeks, celery, sage and thyme plus
salt and pepper.
Cook 5 minutes on medium/low heat.
Add your choice of broth and bring to a
simmer.

In a large bowl, beat 2 eggs and mix in
parsley.
Add bread cubes, nuts and apricots.
Pour in the vegetable mixture from the
skillet and toss.
Transfer to a buttered baking dish and
dot the top with butter.
Cover with foil and bake 30 minutes.
Uncover and continue baking until
golden (approximately an additional
30 minutes).

Note: If you want to finish cooking the
stuffing inside of a turkey or other meat, do so
after the first 30 minutes of covered baking.

Nod to Bourbon Street Stuffing

Kick up your Southern style stuffing with a hit of Bourbon and pecans. The pears in this stuffing add sweetness to the dish which balances the flavors to compliment any entrée. This recipe results in approximately 8 servings.

You will need:

1 large skillet
1 large mixing bowl
1 large baking dish

Ingredients

1 Stick unsalted butter (plus butter to
    coat baking dish and dot the top with)
2 cups onions, diced
2 cups celery, diced
2 firm, medium pears, diced
1 cup pecans, chopped
1 tablespoon sage, minced (or 2
    teaspoons of dried sage)
1 tablespoon thyme, minced (or 2
    teaspoons of dried thyme)
1/2 cup Bourbon
Salt and pepper to taste
3 cups broth (chicken, turkey, vegetable
    as preferred)
2 eggs

1/4 cup parsley, chopped
16 cups of dried bread cubes

Directions

Preheat oven to 375 degrees.

Melt 1 stick of butter in a large skillet
over medium heat.
Add onions, celery, sage and thyme plus
salt and pepper.
Cook 3 minutes on medium/low heat.
Add pecans and Bourbon and simmer for
2 minutes.
Add your choice of broth and bring to a
simmer.

In a large bowl, beat 2 eggs and mix in
parsley.
Add bread cubes. Pour in the vegetable
mixture from the skillet and toss.
Transfer to a buttered baking dish and
dot the top with butter.
Cover with foil and bake 30 minutes.
Uncover and continue baking until
golden (approximately an additional
30 minutes).

Note: If you want to finish cooking the
stuffing inside of a turkey or other meat, do so
after the first 30 minutes of covered baking.

Christmas Chestnut Stuffing

Do Christmas carols have you thinking about roasted chestnuts? This savory and nutty stuffing will hit the spot and is quite universal in pairing with a variety of meats. This recipe results in approximately 8 servings.

You will need:

1 large skillet
1 large mixing bowl
1 large baking dish

Ingredients

1 Stick unsalted butter (plus butter to coat baking dish and dot the top with)
2 cups onions, diced
1/2 cup chestnuts, chopped
2 cups celery, diced
1 tablespoon sage, minced (or 2 teaspoons of dried sage)
1 tablespoon thyme, minced (or 2 teaspoons of dried thyme)
Salt and pepper to taste
3 cups broth (chicken, turkey, vegetable as preferred)
2 eggs
1/4 cup parsley, chopped
16 cups of dried bread cubes

Directions

Preheat oven to 375 degrees.

Melt 1 stick of butter in a large skillet over medium heat.
Add onions, chestnuts, celery, sage and thyme plus salt and pepper.
Cook 5 minutes on medium/low heat.
Add your choice of broth and bring to a simmer.

In a large bowl, beat 2 eggs and mix in parsley.
Add bread cubes. Pour in the vegetable mixture from the skillet and toss.
Transfer to a buttered baking dish and dot the top with butter.
Cover with foil and bake 30 minutes.
Uncover and continue baking until golden (approximately an additional 30 minutes).

Note: If you want to finish cooking the stuffing inside of a turkey or other meat, do so after the first 30 minutes of covered baking.

Mushroom Bonanza Stuffing

For those who love mushrooms, this is the stuffing to try. It is a favorite around my house when serving beef dishes that use a decidedly French flair. This recipe results in approximately 8 servings.

You will need:

1 large skillet
1 large mixing bowl
1 large baking dish

Ingredients

1 Stick unsalted butter (plus butter to
    coat baking dish and dot the top with)
3 bulbs leeks, diced (approximately 3
    cups)
2 cups celery, diced
1 tablespoon rosemary, minced (or 2
    teaspoons of dried rosemary)
1 tablespoon Herbs de Provence
Salt and pepper to taste
3 cups broth (chicken, turkey, vegetable
    as preferred)
2 eggs
1/4 cup parsley, chopped
16 cups of dried bread cubes

1 lb. mushrooms, cleaned and sliced
(works best with a mix of wild
mushrooms)

Directions

Preheat oven to 375 degrees.

Melt 1 stick of butter in a large skillet
over medium heat.
Add leeks, celery, rosemary, Herbs de
Provence and mushrooms plus salt
and pepper.
Cook 5 minutes on medium/low heat.
Add your choice of broth and bring to a
simmer.

In a large bowl, beat 2 eggs and mix in
parsley.
Add bread cubes. Pour in the vegetable
mixture from the skillet and toss.
Transfer to a buttered baking dish and
dot the top with butter.
Cover with foil and bake 30 minutes.
Uncover and continue baking until
golden (approximately an additional
30 minutes).

Note: If you want to finish cooking the
stuffing inside of a turkey or other meat, do so
after the first 30 minutes of covered baking.

Cheesy Spinach Stuffing

This combination of spinach, Gruyere, and mushrooms compliments poultry, pork, and beef entrees. With the added cheesiness, this stuffing sticks to your ribs more than most others do. This recipe results in approximately 8 servings.

You will need:

1 large skillet
1 large mixing bowl
1 large baking dish

Ingredients

1 Stick unsalted butter (plus butter to coat baking dish and dot the top with)
3 bulbs leeks, diced (approximately 3 cups)
2 cups celery, diced
1 lb. mushrooms, cleaned and sliced/diced (My preference is Portobello, but it works with many different types of mushrooms. It's your preference for selection.)
1 tablespoon sage, minced (or 2 teaspoons of dried sage)
1 tablespoon thyme, minced (or 2 teaspoons of dried thyme)

Salt and pepper to taste
3 cups broth (chicken, turkey, vegetable
    as preferred)
2 eggs
1/4 cup parsley, chopped
16 cups of dried bread cubes
6 cups of baby spinach (or 2 cups of
    frozen spinach that has been thawed)
1 cup diced Gruyere cheese

Directions

Preheat oven to 375 degrees.

Melt 1 stick of butter in a large skillet
    over medium heat.
Add leeks, celery, mushrooms, sage and
    thyme plus salt and pepper.
Cook 5 minutes on medium/low heat.
Add your choice of broth and bring to a
    simmer.

In a large bowl, beat 2 eggs and mix in
    parsley.
Add bread cubes, cheese, and spinach.
Pour in the vegetable mixture from the
    skillet and toss.
Transfer to a buttered baking dish and
    dot the top with butter.
Cover with foil and bake 30 minutes.

Uncover and continue baking until
golden (approximately an additional
30 minutes).

Note: If you want to finish cooking the
stuffing inside of a turkey or other meat, do so
after the first 30 minutes of covered baking.

Winter Roasted Veggie Stuffing

This stuffing takes longer than the others to prepare due to the roasting of vegetables, but it is a tasty alternative when serving limited side dishes at your holiday gathering. It is in essence two dishes in one. This recipe results in approximately 8 servings by halving the bread used.

You will need:

1 large roasting pan or baking sheet
1 large skillet
1 large mixing bowl
1 large baking dish

Ingredients

Vegetable or olive oil to coat vegetables
    while roasting
2 cups butternut squash, diced
2 cups carrots, diced
2 cups parsnips, diced
1 medium red onion, diced
1 Stick unsalted butter (plus butter to
    coat baking dish and dot the top with)
2 cups onions, diced
2 cups celery, diced
1 tablespoon sage, minced (or 2
    teaspoons of dried sage)

1 tablespoon thyme, minced (or 2
    teaspoons of dried thyme)
Salt and pepper to taste
3 cups broth (chicken, turkey, vegetable
    as preferred)
2 eggs
1/4 cup parsley, chopped
8 cups of dried bread cubes

Directions

Preheat oven to 400 degrees.

Coat butternut, carrots, parsnips, and red
    onions in oil. The easiest way to do
    this is to combine 2 tablespoons of oil
    with vegetables in a sealable bag and
    shake.
Place in a single layer on a baking sheet
    or in a large roasting dish.
Roast approximately 25 minutes, until
    vegetables are golden.
Remove from oven and set aside.

Heat oven to 375 degrees.

Melt 1 stick of butter in a large skillet
    over medium heat.
Add onions, celery, sage and thyme plus
    salt and pepper.
Cook 5 minutes on medium/low heat.

Add your choice of broth and bring to a
simmer.

In a large bowl, beat 2 eggs and mix in
parsley.
Add bread cubes. Pour in the vegetable
mixture from the skillet and toss.
Add roasted vegetables and mix
thoroughly.
Transfer to a buttered baking dish and
dot the top with butter.
Cover with foil and bake 30 minutes.
Uncover and continue baking until
golden (approximately an additional
30 minutes).

Note: If you want to finish cooking the
stuffing inside of a turkey or other meat, do so
after the first 30 minutes of covered baking.

Onion Overload Stuffing

This stuffing works with any main course and is a favorite of onion lovers everywhere. It combines caramelized sweet onions with the shallots and scallions. This recipe results in approximately 8 servings.

You will need:

1 large skillet
1 large mixing bowl
1 large baking dish

Ingredients

1 stick unsalted butter (plus butter to coat baking dish and dot the top with)
2 cups sweet onions, diced
2 cups celery, diced
1 tablespoon sage, minced (or 2 teaspoons of dried sage)
1 tablespoon thyme seasoning
Salt and pepper to taste
3 cups broth (chicken, turkey, vegetable as preferred)
2 eggs
1/4 cup parsley, chopped
1 cup shallots, minced
1 tablespoon garlic, minced
1 1/4 cups scallions, chopped

16 cups of dried bread cubes (Sourdough is a personal favorite for this one)

Directions

Preheat oven to 375 degrees.

Melt stick of butter in a large skillet over medium heat.
Add onions, celery, sage and thyme plus salt and pepper.
Cook 3 minutes on medium/low heat.
Add shallots and cook an additional 2 minutes
Add your choice of broth and bring to a simmer.

In a large bowl, beat 2 eggs and mix in parsley.
Add bread cubes, garlic, and 1 cup of scallions.
Pour in the vegetable mixture from the skillet and toss.
Transfer to a buttered baking dish and dot the top with butter.
Cover with foil and bake 30 minutes.
Uncover and continue baking until golden (approximately an additional 30 minutes).

Top by sprinkling remaining 1/4 cup of
scallions over the dish before serving.

Note: If you want to finish cooking the
stuffing inside of a turkey or other meat, do so
after the first 30 minutes of covered baking.

Pear-Pecan Cornbread Stuffing

When you want a sweeter stuffing to compliment a saltier main course, this sweet cornbread stuffing is a crowd-pleaser. This stuffing combines pears, pecans, and dates with the texture of cornbread. If you want to add a salty component to balance out the dish on its own, add 1/2 pound of crumbled bacon to the vegetable sauté. This recipe results in approximately 8 servings.

You will need:

1 large skillet
1 large mixing bowl
1 large baking dish

Ingredients

1 stick unsalted butter (plus butter to coat
    baking dish and dot the top with)
2 cups onions, diced
2 cups celery, diced
1 tablespoon sage, minced (or 2
    teaspoons of dried sage)
1 tablespoon thyme
Salt and pepper to taste
3 cups broth (chicken, turkey, vegetable
    as preferred)
2 eggs

1/4 cup parsley, chopped

2-3 medium to large pears, diced (2 cups worth)

3/4 cup dates, diced

1/2 cup pecans, chopped

6 cups of cornbread cubes, dried

8 cups of white bread cubes, dried

Directions

Preheat oven to 375 degrees.

Melt 1 stick of butter in a large skillet over medium heat.

Add onions, celery, sage and thyme plus salt and pepper.

Cook 5 minutes on medium/low heat.

Add your choice of broth and bring to a simmer.

In a large bowl, beat 2 eggs and mix in parsley.

Add bread cubes, pears, dates, and pecans.

Pour in the vegetable mixture from the skillet and toss.

Transfer to a buttered baking dish and dot the top with butter.

Cover with foil and bake 30 minutes.

Uncover and continue baking until
golden (approximately an additional
30 minutes).

Note: If you want to finish cooking the
stuffing inside of a turkey or other meat, do so
after the first 30 minutes of covered baking.

Sausage Stuffing Recipes

The following collection of recipes features the use of sausage. Most commonly, pork sausage is used in stuffing recipes, but other options such as turkey sausage can be used as a substitute. If you enjoy or desire a spicier stuffing, Italian sausage (without the casing) can also be used. The final recipes in this section highlight the use of chorizo, which is often referred to as "Mexican sausage".

Classic Sausage Stuffing

You can modify this meaty stuffing classic a variety of ways based on the type of sausage that you use. For turkey dinners, I use sage sausage to further compliment the poultry while doubling the thyme in the recipe. If you want a spicier stuffing, using a hot version of sausage will add a kick. Of course, you can keep it simple with the traditional sausage. This recipe results in approximately 8 servings. Note: this recipe uses less butter than other stuffing recipes in this book.

You will need:

1 large skillet
1 large mixing bowl
1 large baking dish

Ingredients

1 lb. sausage of choice (16 oz. chub)
6 tablespoons unsalted butter (plus butter to coat baking dish and dot the top with)
2 cups onions, diced
2 cups celery, diced

1 tablespoon sage, minced (or 2
   teaspoons of dried sage)
1 tablespoon thyme, minced (or 2
   teaspoons of dried thyme)
Salt and pepper to taste
3 cups broth (chicken, turkey, vegetable
   as preferred)
2 eggs
1/4 cup parsley, chopped
16 cups of dried bread cubes

Directions

Preheat oven to 375 degrees.

Brown sausage into crumbles in a large
   skillet over medium heat.
Melt 6 tablespoons of butter into the
   sausage crumbles.
Add onions, celery, sage and thyme plus
   salt and pepper.
Cook 5 minutes on medium/low heat.
Add your choice of broth and bring to a
   simmer.

In a large bowl, beat 2 eggs and mix in
   parsley.
Add bread cubes. Pour in the vegetable-
   sausage mixture from the skillet and
   toss.

Transfer to a buttered baking dish and
dot the top with butter.
Cover with foil and bake 30 minutes.
Uncover and continue baking until
golden (approximately an additional
30 minutes).

Note: If you want to finish cooking the
stuffing inside of a turkey or other meat, do so
after the first 30 minutes of covered baking.

Meaty Apple Stuffing

This stuffing combines sausage with apples for colder weather dish that also works well with Easter hams. This recipe results in approximately 8 servings.

You will need:

1 large skillet
1 large mixing bowl
1 large baking dish

Ingredients

1 lb. sausage of choice (16 oz. chub)
6 tablespoons unsalted butter (plus butter to coat baking dish and dot the top with)
2 cups onions, diced
1 cup celery, diced
1 bulb fennel, diced (approximately one cup)
2 medium apples, diced
1 tablespoon sage, minced (or 2 teaspoons of dried sage)
1 tablespoon thyme, minced (or 2 teaspoons of dried thyme)
1 teaspoon, fennel seeds
Salt and pepper to taste

3 cups broth (chicken, turkey, vegetable as preferred)
2 eggs
1/4 cup parsley, chopped
16 cups of dried bread cubes

Directions

Preheat oven to 375 degrees.

Brown sausage and melt 1 stick of butter in a large skillet over medium heat.
Add onions, celery, fennel, apples, fennel seeds, sage and thyme plus salt and pepper.
Cook 5 minutes on medium/low heat.
Add your choice of broth and bring to a simmer.

In a large bowl, beat 2 eggs and mix in parsley.
Add bread cubes. Pour in the sausage-vegetable mixture from the skillet and toss.
Transfer to a buttered baking dish and dot the top with butter.
Cover with foil and bake 30 minutes.
Uncover and continue baking until golden (approximately an additional 30 minutes).

Note: If you want to finish cooking the stuffing inside of a turkey or other meat, do so after the first 30 minutes of covered baking.

Onion Apple Sausage Stuffing

This stuffing has a hint of sweetness combined with the savory sausage which makes this a solid compliment to pork-based main dishes as well as dark meat turkey. This recipe results in approximately 8 servings.

You will need:

1 large skillet
1 large mixing bowl
1 large baking dish

Ingredients

1 lb. sage sausage (16 oz. chub)
6 tablespoons unsalted butter (plus butter to coat baking dish and dot the top with)
2 cups onions, diced
2 cups celery, diced
1 tablespoon sage, minced (or 2 teaspoons of dried sage)
1 tablespoon thyme
Salt and pepper to taste
3 cups broth (chicken, turkey, vegetable as preferred)
2 eggs
1/4 cup parsley, chopped

16 cups of dried bread cubes (Sourdough is a personal favorite for this one)
2 cups scallions, chopped
2 large apples, diced (McIntosh works well for this one)

Directions

Preheat oven to 375 degrees.

Brown sausage into crumbles in a large skillet and melt 6 tablespoons of butter into the meat.

Add onions, celery, sage and thyme plus salt and pepper.

Cook 5 minutes on medium/low heat.

Add your choice of broth and bring to a simmer.

In a large bowl, beat 2 eggs and mix in parsley.

Add bread cubes, apples, and scallions (reserve 1/4 of scallions for topping).

Pour in the vegetable mixture from the skillet and toss.

Transfer to a buttered baking dish and dot the top with butter.

Cover with foil and bake 30 minutes.

Uncover and continue baking until golden (approximately an additional 30 minutes).

Sprinkle remaining scallions over the top before serving.

Note: If you want to finish cooking the stuffing inside of a turkey or other meat, do so after the first 30 minutes of covered baking.

Sunny and Spicy Sausage Stuffing

The sweetness of sun dried tomatoes combines with the kick of hot Italian sausage to provide a mouthful of goodness that will make you want to grab the next flight to Tuscany. This recipe results in approximately 8 servings.

You will need:

1 large skillet
1 large mixing bowl
1 large baking dish

Ingredients

1 lb. hot Italian sausage (16 oz. chub)
6 tablespoons unsalted butter (plus butter to coat baking dish and dot the top with)
2 cups onions, diced
2 cups celery, diced
1 tablespoon sage, minced (or 2 teaspoons of dried sage)
1 tablespoon Italian seasoning
Salt and pepper to taste
3 cups broth (chicken, turkey, vegetable as preferred)
2 eggs
1/4 cup parsley, chopped

16 cups of dried bread cubes (Sourdough
is a personal favorite for this one)
1 cup sundried tomatoes, diced

Directions

Preheat oven to 375 degrees.

Brown sausage into crumbles in a large
skillet and melt 6 tablespoons of
butter into the meat.
Add onions, celery, sage and Italian
seasoning plus salt and pepper.
Cook 5 minutes on medium/low heat.
Add your choice of broth and bring to a
simmer.

In a large bowl, beat 2 eggs and mix in
parsley.
Add bread cubes and sundried tomatoes.
Pour in the vegetable mixture from the
skillet and toss.
Transfer to a buttered baking dish and
dot the top with butter.
Cover with foil and bake 30 minutes.
Uncover and continue baking until
golden (approximately an additional
30 minutes).

Note: If you want to finish cooking the stuffing inside of a turkey or other meat, do so after the first 30 minutes of covered baking.

Sausage Spinach Cornbread Stuffing

This stuffing combines protein, vegetables, dairy and carbs into a filling side dish that can be enjoyed on its own as well as complimenting your holiday meal. The ingredients combine into a complex and tasty mouthful with every bite. This recipe results in approximately 8 servings.

You will need:

1 large skillet
1 large mixing bowl
1 large baking dish

Ingredients

1 lb. sausage (16 oz. chub)
1 stick of unsalted butter (plus butter to
    coat baking dish and dot the top with)
2 cups onions, diced
2 cups celery, diced
1 tablespoon sage, minced (or 2
    teaspoons of dried sage)
1 tablespoon Italian seasoning
Salt and pepper to taste
3 cups broth (chicken, turkey, vegetable
    as preferred)
4 cups of chopped baby spinach (or 2
    cups of frozen spinach, thawed)

2 eggs

1/4 cup parsley, chopped

6 cups of cornbread cubes, dried

8 cups of white bread cubes, dried
(Sourdough is a personal favorite for this one)

1/3 cup of toasted pine nuts

1/4 cup of Parmesan cheese

Directions

Preheat oven to 375 degrees.

Brown sausage into crumbles in a large skillet and melt stick of butter into the meat.

Add onions, celery, sage and Italian seasoning plus salt and pepper.

Cook 5 minutes on medium/low heat.

Add your choice of broth and spinach. Bring to a simmer.

In a large bowl, beat 2 eggs and mix in parsley.

Add bread cubes and pine nuts.

Pour in the vegetable mixture from the skillet and toss.

Transfer to a buttered baking dish and dot the top with butter.

Cover with foil and bake 30 minutes.

Uncover and continue baking until
golden (approximately an additional
30 minutes).

Top with Parmesan after removing from
oven.

Note: If you want to finish cooking the
stuffing inside of a turkey or other meat, do so
after the first 30 minutes of covered baking. In
this case, you will skip topping with Parmesan
cheese.

Chorizo Stuffing

Take the classic sausage stuffing south of the border with this spicy alternative using chorizo. For those that are vegetarian, a soy based chorizo product can be substituted, but the initial browning step should be changed to a brief chop of the chub shaped product. Extended cooking of the soy chorizo will result in a mealy consistency. This recipe results in approximately 8 servings.

You will need:

1 large skillet
1 large mixing bowl
1 large baking dish

Ingredients

1 lb. Chorizo or soy Chorizo (16 oz. chub)
6 tablespoons unsalted butter (plus butter to coat baking dish and dot the top with)
2 cups onions, diced
2 cups celery, diced
1 tablespoon thyme
1 tablespoon oregano, minced (keep the full tablespoon with dried oregano as well)

Salt and pepper to taste

3 cups broth (chicken, turkey, vegetable as preferred)

2 eggs

1/4 cup parsley, chopped

16 cups of dried bread cubes (Sourdough is a personal favorite for this one)

1 cup sundried tomatoes, diced

Directions

Preheat oven to 375 degrees.

Brown the chorizo into crumbles in a large skillet and melt 6 tablespoons of butter into the meat.

Add onions, celery, thyme and oregano plus salt and pepper.

Cook 5 minutes on medium/low heat.

Add your choice of broth and bring to a simmer.

In a large bowl, beat 2 eggs and mix in parsley.

Add bread cubes.

Pour in the vegetable mixture from the skillet and toss.

Transfer to a buttered baking dish and dot the top with butter.

Cover with foil and bake 30 minutes.

Uncover and continue baking until
  golden (approximately an additional
  30 minutes).

Note: If you want to finish cooking the stuffing inside of a turkey or other meat, do so after the first 30 minutes of covered baking.

Sophisticated Chorizo Stuffing

Consider this the gourmet version of the familiar chorizo stuffing with the addition of manchego cheese and dates. This stuffing really pops when sourdough bread cubes are used. This recipe results in approximately 8 servings.

You will need:

1 large skillet
1 large mixing bowl
1 large baking dish

Ingredients

1 lb. chorizo or soy chorizo (16 oz. chub)
6 tablespoons unsalted butter (plus butter to coat baking dish and dot the top with)
2 cups onions, diced
2 cups celery, diced
1 tablespoon oregano, minced (same for dried)
Salt and pepper to taste
3 cups broth (chicken, turkey, vegetable as preferred)
2 eggs
1/4 cup parsley, chopped
16 cups of dried bread cubes (Sourdough is recommended)

1 cup dates, chopped
1/2 cup manchego cheese, cubed

Directions

Preheat oven to 375 degrees.

Brown chorizo into crumbles in a large
    skillet and melt 6 tablespoons of
    butter into the meat.
Add onions, celery, oregano plus salt and
    pepper.
Cook 5 minutes on medium/low heat.
Add your choice of broth and bring to a
    simmer.

In a large bowl, beat 2 eggs and mix in
    parsley.
Add bread cubes, dates, and cheese.
Pour in the vegetable mixture from the
    skillet and toss.
Transfer to a buttered baking dish and
    dot the top with butter.
Cover with foil and bake 30 minutes.
Uncover and continue baking until
    golden (approximately an additional
    30 minutes).

Note: If you want to finish cooking the
stuffing inside of a turkey or other meat, do so
after the first 30 minutes of covered baking.

Stuffing Recipes Using Other Meat Options

The follow selection of stuffing recipes includes meats that are not the more typical sausage options. The recipes include choices using pancetta, prosciutto, ham, bacon, and oysters. Technically, the recipes using Kielbasa and Andouille sausage could be included under the sausage section, but the logic for placing them here is that they are not the "traditional" sausage fare that is expected in stuffing. Either way, these recipes give you the opportunity to introduce something new to your dinner table.

Pan-Chestnut Stuffing

Instead of using sausage, this recipe uses pancetta and chestnuts to highlight the use of semolina bread for a stuffing good enough to accompany any entrée at your holiday table. This recipe results in approximately 8 servings.

You will need:

1 large skillet
1 large mixing bowl
1 large baking dish

Ingredients

1 lb. diced pancetta
6 tablespoons unsalted butter (plus butter to coat baking dish and dot the top with)
2 cups onions, diced
1 ½ cups chestnuts, chopped
2 cups celery, diced
1 tablespoon sage, minced (or 2 teaspoons of dried sage)
1 tablespoon Italian seasoning
Salt and pepper to taste
3 cups broth (chicken, turkey, vegetable as preferred)
2 eggs
1/4 cup parsley, chopped

16 cups of dried bread cubes (Semolina bread is advised)

Directions

Preheat oven to 375 degrees.

Warm and crisp pancetta while melting 6 tablespoons of butter into a large skillet.
Add onions, chestnuts, celery, sage and Italian seasoning plus salt and pepper.
Cook 5 minutes on medium/low heat.
Add your choice of broth and bring to a simmer.

In a large bowl, beat 2 eggs and mix in parsley.
Add bread cubes.
Pour in the vegetable mixture from the skillet and toss.
Transfer to a buttered baking dish and dot the top with butter.
Cover with foil and bake 30 minutes.
Uncover and continue baking until golden (approximately an additional 30 minutes).

Note: If you want to finish cooking the stuffing inside of a turkey or other meat, do so after the first 30 minutes of covered baking.

Butternut Pan or Pro Stuffing

Butternut squash partners with either pancetta or prosciutto (or both) in this mouthwatering stuffing that is guaranteed to become a holiday favorite. It takes a little extra time if you choose to roast the butternut to soften it before peeling and dicing. This recipe results in approximately 8 servings.

You will need:

1 baking dish, big enough for butternut squash
1 large skillet
1 large mixing bowl
1 large baking dish

Ingredients

1 butternut squash, at least 1 lb. (peeled and diced)
1 lb. pancetta or prosciutto, diced (you can do a 1/2 lb. of each as an alternative)
6 tablespoons unsalted butter (plus butter to coat baking dish and dot the top with)
2 cups onions, diced
2 cups celery, diced

1 tablespoon sage, minced (or 2
  teaspoons of dried sage)
1 tablespoon thyme (or 2 teaspoons dried
  thyme)
Salt and pepper to taste
3 cups broth (chicken, turkey, vegetable
  as preferred)
2 eggs
1/4 cup parsley, chopped
16 cups of dried bread cubes

Directions

*To soften butternut squash before peeling
  and dicing (optional)*
Preheat oven to 400 degrees.

Cut the butternut squash in half and
  remove insides.
Put a 1/2 inch of water in bottom of
  baking dish.
Place butternut squash halves in baking
  dish, with cut side down.
Roast for approximately 25 minutes to
  soften.
Remove and let cool before dicing

Stuffing
Heat oven to 375 degrees

Brown and crisp meat in a large skillet and add 6 tablespoons of butter until melted.

Add onions, celery, squash, sage and thyme plus salt and pepper.

Cook 5 minutes on medium/low heat.

Add your choice of broth and bring to a simmer.

In a large bowl, beat 2 eggs and mix in parsley.

Add bread cubes.

Pour in the vegetable mixture from the skillet and toss.

Transfer to a buttered baking dish and dot the top with butter.

Cover with foil and bake 30 minutes.

Uncover and continue baking until golden (approximately an additional 30 minutes).

Note: If you want to finish cooking the stuffing inside of a turkey or other meat, do so after the first 30 minutes of covered baking.

Pan-caccia Stuffing

The sweet surprise of raisiny sweetness is a palate-pleasing contrast to the combination of pancetta, rosemary, and focaccia bread. This stuffing works well for pork, beef and poultry meals. This recipe results in approximately 8 servings.

You will need:

1 large skillet
1 large mixing bowl
1 large baking dish

Ingredients

1 lb. diced pancetta, diced
6 tablespoons unsalted butter (plus butter to coat baking dish and dot the top with)
2 cups onions, diced
1 bulb fennel, diced (approximately 1 cup)
2 tablespoon rosemary, minced (or 1 teaspoon of dried rosemary)
Salt and pepper to taste
3 cups broth (chicken, turkey, vegetable as preferred)
2 eggs
1/4 cup parsley, chopped

16 cups of dried bread cubes (Focaccia bread)
2 cups golden raisins

Directions

Preheat oven to 375 degrees.

Crisp and brown pancetta with 6 tablespoons of butter in a large skillet.
Add onions, fennel, rosemary plus salt and pepper.
Cook 5 minutes on medium/low heat.
Add your choice of broth and bring to a simmer.

In a large bowl, beat 2 eggs and mix in parsley.
Add bread cubes and raisins.
Pour in the vegetable mixture from the skillet and toss.
Transfer to a buttered baking dish and dot the top with butter.
Cover with foil and bake 30 minutes.
Uncover and continue baking until golden (approximately an additional 30 minutes).

Note: If you want to finish cooking the stuffing inside of a turkey or other meat, do so after the first 30 minutes of covered baking.

Country Ham Cornbread Stuffing

Ham and cornbread go hand-in-hand, and this stuffing features this dynamic duo. The introduction of scallions into the mix provides an eye catching element to this dish. This recipe results in approximately 8 servings.

You will need:

1 large skillet
1 large mixing bowl
1 large baking dish

Ingredients

2 cups diced ham
1 stick of unsalted butter (plus butter to coat baking dish and dot the top with)
1 cup onions, diced
1 cup scallions, chopped
2 cups celery, diced
1 tablespoon sage, minced (or 2 teaspoons of dried sage)
1 tablespoon thyme
Salt and pepper to taste
3 cups broth (chicken, turkey, vegetable as preferred)
2 eggs
1/4 cup parsley, chopped
6 cups cornbread cubes, dried

8 cups white bread cubes, dried

Directions

Preheat oven to 375 degrees.

Melt stick of butter in a large skillet over
    medium heat.
Add onions, celery, sage and thyme plus
    salt and pepper.
Cook 5 minutes on medium/low heat.
Add your choice of broth and bring to a
    simmer.

In a large bowl, beat 2 eggs and mix in
    parsley.
Add all of the bread cubes, ham, and
    scallions.
Pour in the vegetable mixture from the
    skillet and toss.
Transfer to a buttered baking dish and
    dot the top with butter.
Cover with foil and bake 30 minutes.
Uncover and continue baking until
    golden (approximately an additional
    30 minutes).

Note: If you want to finish cooking the
stuffing inside of a turkey or other meat, do so
after the first 30 minutes of covered baking.

Ham-Mustard Cornbread Stuffing

Add a dimension to the Ham Cornbread stuffing with the introduction of mustard tanginess. With the added potency of the mustard, the sage in this recipe is replaced with rosemary. This recipe results in approximately 8 servings.

You will need:

1 large skillet
1 large mixing bowl
1 large baking dish

Ingredients

1 lb. ham, diced
6 tablespoons unsalted butter (plus butter to coat baking dish and dot the top with)
2 cups onions, diced
2 cups celery, diced
1 tablespoon rosemary, minced (or 2 teaspoons of dried rosemary)
1 tablespoon thyme
Salt and pepper to taste
3 cups broth (chicken, turkey, vegetable as preferred)
1/4 cup course Dijon mustard
2 eggs

1/4 cup parsley, chopped
6 cups cornbread cubes, dried
8 cups white bread cubes, dried

Directions

Preheat oven to 375 degrees.

Combine ham and 6 tablespoons of
butter in a large skillet until warmed
and melted.
Add onions, celery, sage and rosemary
plus salt and pepper.
Cook 5 minutes on medium/low heat.
Add your choice of broth and mustard.
Bring to a simmer.

In a large bowl, beat 2 eggs and mix in
parsley.
Add all bread cubes.
Pour in the vegetable mixture from the
skillet and toss.
Transfer to a buttered baking dish and
dot the top with butter.
Cover with foil and bake 30 minutes.
Uncover and continue baking until
golden (approximately an additional
30 minutes).

Note: If you want to finish cooking the stuffing inside of a turkey or other meat, do so after the first 30 minutes of covered baking.

Bacon-Pepper Jack Cornbread Stuffing

I have to admit, this is one of my personal favorites with the combination of bacon goodness, pepper kick, cheesiness, and cornbread sweetness. I love serving this with beef entrees, but it goes well with all types of meats. This recipe results in approximately 8 servings.

You will need:

1 large skillet
1 large mixing bowl
1 large baking dish

Ingredients

1/2 lb. bacon
6 tablespoons unsalted butter (plus butter to coat baking dish and dot the top with)
2 cups onions, diced
2 cups celery, diced
1 tablespoon sage, minced (or 2 teaspoons of dried sage)
1 tablespoon thyme
Salt and pepper to taste

3 cups broth (chicken, turkey, vegetable
   as preferred)
2 eggs
1/4 cup parsley, chopped
1 serrano pepper, sliced (for a milder
   flavor remove seeds and veins)
6 cups of cornbread cubes, dried
8 cups of white bread cubes, dried
2 cups of diced/cubed pepper jack cheese

Directions

Preheat oven to 375 degrees.

Using a pair of cooking scissors, cut the
   slices of bacon in bite-sized pieces
   and cook in a large skillet.
Once the bacon is cooked, melt 6
   tablespoons of butter into the meat.
Add onions, celery, sage and thyme plus
   salt and pepper.
Cook 5 minutes on medium/low heat.
Add your choice of broth and bring to a
   simmer. Add serrano peppers.

In a large bowl, beat 2 eggs and mix in
   parsley.
Add all bread cubes and pepper jack
   cheese. Mix thoroughly.
Pour in the bacon-vegetable mixture
   from the skillet and toss.

Transfer to a buttered baking dish and
dot the top with butter.
Cover with foil and bake 30 minutes.
Uncover and continue baking until
golden (approximately an additional
30 minutes).

Note: If you want to finish cooking the
stuffing inside of a turkey or other meat, do so
after the first 30 minutes of covered baking.

Bayou Cornbread Stuffing

The bayou lives in this Cajun inspired cornbread stuffing. Andouille sausage mixes with okra, and the holy trinity of Creole cooking (onions, bell peppers, and celery) may have New Orleans calling your name by the end of your meal. This recipe results in approximately 8 servings.

You will need:

1 large skillet
1 large mixing bowl
1 large baking dish

Ingredients

1 lb. Andouille sausage
1 stick of unsalted butter (plus butter to coat baking dish and dot the top with)
2 cups onions, diced
2 cups celery, diced
1 cup red bell pepper, diced
1 cup green bell pepper, diced
1 tablespoon sage, minced (or 2 teaspoons of dried sage)
1 tablespoon thyme
Salt and pepper to taste
Pinch of cayenne pepper

3 cups broth (chicken, turkey, vegetable as preferred)
1 1/2 cups okra, sliced
2 eggs
1/4 cup parsley, chopped
6 cups of cornbread cubes, dried
8 cups of white bread cubes, dried

Directions

Preheat oven to 375 degrees.

Cook sausage in a large skillet. Let cool to slice into bite-sized pieces.
Return sausage to skillet and melt into crumbles in a large skillet and melt stick of butter.
Add onions, celery, bell peppers, sage, thyme and pinch of cayenne pepper plus salt and pepper.
Cook 5 minutes on medium/low heat.
Add your choice of broth and bring to a simmer.

In a large bowl, beat 2 eggs and mix in parsley.
Add bread cubes and sliced okra.
Pour in the vegetable mixture from the skillet and toss.
Transfer to a buttered baking dish and dot the top with butter.

Cover with foil and bake 30 minutes.
Uncover and continue baking until
golden (approximately an additional
30 minutes).

Note: If you want to finish cooking the stuffing inside of a turkey or other meat, do so after the first 30 minutes of covered baking.

From Krakow with Love Kielbasa Stuffing

This is a stuffing that is the product of my travels. Though named for the Polish city, similarly styled dishes can be found in Prague and surrounding areas as well. The use of sauerkraut may throw some off from trying this stuffing, but the vinegar kick in the sauerkraut softens during baking. This recipe results in approximately 8 servings.

You will need:

1 large skillet
1 large mixing bowl
1 large baking dish

Ingredients

1 lb. of Kielbasa, sliced and diced
1 stick unsalted butter (plus butter to coat baking dish and dot the top with)
2 cups onions, diced
1lb sauerkraut, rinsed and lightly patted dry
2 cups celery, diced
1 tablespoon sage, minced (or 2 teaspoons of dried sage)

1 tablespoon thyme, minced (or 2
   teaspoons of dried thyme)
2 teaspoons paprika
Salt and pepper to taste
3 cups broth (chicken, turkey, vegetable
   as preferred)
2 eggs
1/4 cup parsley, chopped
16 cups of dried bread cubes

Directions

Preheat oven to 375 degrees.

Brown Kielbasa in a large skillet over
   medium heat. Add 6 tablespoons of
   butter.
Add onions, celery, sage, thyme, paprika,
   and sauerkraut plus salt and pepper.
Cook 5 minutes on medium/low heat.
Add your choice of broth and bring to a
   simmer.

In a large bowl, beat 2 eggs and mix in
   parsley.
Add bread cubes. Pour in the vegetable
   mixture from the skillet and toss.
Transfer to a buttered baking dish and
   dot the top with butter.
Cover with foil and bake 30 minutes.

Uncover and continue baking until
    golden (approximately an additional
    30 minutes).

Note: If you want to finish cooking the
stuffing inside of a turkey or other meat, do so
after the first 30 minutes of covered baking.

Oyster Stuffing

This stuffing is a topic of debate around our holiday table. Some members love it with potato bread while others prefer an extra sourdough. It's your call as to the direction you want your dish to go. A sweeter taste to balance out the oyster saltiness requires potato bread. For those who want a touch of San Francisco to go with the sea flavor, sourdough is the way to go. This is a taste treat for a bit of surf and turf for meals featuring beef dishes. This recipe results in approximately 8 servings.

You will need:

1 large skillet
1 large mixing bowl
1 large baking dish

Ingredients

1 Stick unsalted butter (plus butter to coat baking dish and dot the top with)
2 cups onions, diced
2 cups celery, diced
1 tablespoon Old Bay seasoning
2 teaspoons thyme, minced (or 2 teaspoons of dried thyme)
Salt and pepper to taste

3 cups broth (chicken, turkey, vegetable as preferred)
1/4 cup Vermouth, dry
1/2 cup oyster juice
2 eggs
1/4 cup parsley, chopped
16 cups of dried bread cubes
1 lb. oysters, shucked

Directions

Preheat oven to 375 degrees.

Melt 1 stick of butter in a large skillet over medium heat.
Add onions, celery, Old Bay and thyme plus salt and pepper.
Cook 5 minutes on medium/low heat.
Add your choice of broth, Vermouth, and oyster juice. Bring to a simmer.

In a large bowl, beat 2 eggs and mix in parsley.
Add bread cubes and oysters.
Pour in the vegetable mixture from the skillet and toss.
Transfer to a buttered baking dish and dot the top with butter.
Cover with foil and bake 30 minutes.

Uncover and continue baking until
golden (approximately an additional
30 minutes).

Note: If you want to finish cooking the
stuffing inside of a turkey or other meat, do so
after the first 30 minutes of covered baking.

Vegan Stuffing

This vegan-friendly stuffing is created without the use of butter or eggs. It substitutes oil (vegetable or olive oil) for butter. It can be served as a stand-alone stuffing or as a vegan base to other vegetarian-friendly options in this book. This recipe results in approximately 8 servings.

You will need:

1 large skillet
1 large mixing bowl
1 large baking dish

Ingredients

2 cups of hot, freshly brewed green tea (2 tea bags steeped for 5 minutes)
4-5 tablespoons of oil (vegetable or olive)
2 cups onions, diced
2 cups celery, diced
1 cup mushrooms, sliced (Portobello are a personal favorite, but they need to be diced too)
1 tablespoon garlic, minced
1 tablespoon sage, minced (or 2 teaspoons of dried sage)
1 tablespoon thyme
Salt and pepper to taste
3 cups broth (vegetable)
1/2 cup parsley, chopped
16 cups of dried bread cubes (Sourdough is a personal favorite for this one)

Directions

Preheat oven to 375 degrees.

Heat 3-4 tablespoons of oil in a large skillet over medium heat.
Add onions, celery, sage and thyme plus salt and pepper.

Sautee 3-4 minutes to soften.

Add mushrooms, garlic, sage, and thyme plus salt and pepper.

Cook an additional 3-4 minutes to soften the mushrooms.

Add green tea and return to simmer.

In a large bowl, mix together half of the parsley with all of the bread cubes.

Pour in the contents of the skillet and toss.

Let the mixture sit 8-12 minutes to allow the juices to soak into the bread cubes.

Transfer to an oiled baking dish.

Cover with foil and bake 30 minutes.

Uncover and continue baking until golden (approximately an additional 30 minutes).

Top with remaining parsley and serve.

Note: If you want to finish cooking the stuffing inside of a turkey or other meat, do so after the first 30 minutes of covered baking.

Conclusion

There you have it…a month's worth of stuffing options that work with the full range of holiday menus from Thanksgiving turkey to holiday roasts and Easter ham. Even if you are entertaining those who prefer to skip the meat, recipe options for vegetarians abound, and the last stuffing recipe is designed specifically for those that are vegan. Whether you keep your stuffing simple or make it a gourmet delight, you can rest assured your holiday meal will be memorable for all.

Though this book is written to target holiday stuffing for holiday feasts, there is no reason to limit your enjoyment of these recipes to only major events. Stuffing can make any meal tastier and more filling. They don't need to be limited to being presented as a side either.

Do you love a big stuffed pork chop? How about creating a stuffed pork roast that is slow-cooked and easy? Ever tried stuffed salmon? You can do a variety of stuffed dishes any time of the year by cutting the recipe in half and placing the mixture inside of your meat of choice. Prepare the stuffing according to the recipes listed. Instead of baking the mixture in the oven, baking will be completed within the meat you are preparing.

For those looking for stuffings or dressings that are not bread-based, please check out my *Holiday Dressings: Leave the Bread Behind* book or the holiday super pack *Stuffings, Dressings & Sides: Recipes for Any Holiday Meal.* With the super pack, you get the stuffings, the dressings, and a wide variety of side dishes that work for events year-around…even those that are focused on grilling in the summer months instead of roasting and baking in the cooler seasons.

I hope you have found some old favorites as well as new delights to try. These recipes can be tailored to your specific tastes by including additional ingredients that you enjoy. Once you master the basic recipes, it is easy to modify the selections. Part of the fun of stuffing is that it is easy and relatively inexpensive to experiment with, so have some fun of your own. If you find a new way to make a stuffing delight, I'd love to hear about it. You can find me on Twitter via @GinaLynnYummies.

Please take a moment to leave a short review wherever you purchased this book. If you've found it helpful, you can help others find value in this book as well.

Don't forget...if you haven't already gotten the free stuffing bonus as my personal thank you for purchasing this book, please visit:

www.synchron8publishing.com/GLStuffIt

Thanks again, and happy eats and drinks to all!

About Synchron8 Publishing

Gina Lynn is one of the writers associated with Synchron8 Publishing. We are part micro-publisher and part author- collective, supporting those who have a passion for the written word in its various forms. Our authors work together to create pieces of their own as well as to help promote the works of others. Writers benefit from Synchron8 Publishing resources whether they decide to self-publish or to go a more conventional publishing route.

We continue to expand and grow with new titles regularly announced. Our fiction line is launching a Flash Fiction contest in early

2015. Prizes include publishing opportunities for both a group anthology as well as a potential publishing contract to be the feature author in upcoming books in our Flash 40 and Flash 14 series.

Our catalogue includes: cookbooks, informational books, non-fiction, and various types of fiction.

Learn more at
www.synchron8publishing.com

** synchron8**
Publishing

Titles by Gina Lynn

Current &Upcoming Releases

Mac and Cheese: Quick and Easy Comfort

Stuff It! Leave Boxed Stuffing Behind Forever

Holiday Dressings: Leave the Bread Behind

Holiday Sides 911: Side Dishes for Any Occasion

Stuffings, Dressings & Sides: Recipes for Any Holiday Meal

What Now? Options for Holiday Leftovers

Sensational Sangrias

Mimosagrias

www.ingramcontent.com/pod-product-compliance
Lightning Source LLC
Chambersburg PA
CBHW071608040426
42452CB00008B/1275